TIME
&
MONEY

Books by William Matthews

TIME
&
MONEY

NEW POEMS

WILLIAM MATTHEWS

Houghton Mifflin Company

BOSTON   NEW YORK

For information about permission to reproduce selections from this book, write to Permissions, Houghton Mifflin Company, 215 Park Avenue South, New York, New York 10003.

Library of Congress Cataloging-in-Publication Data
Matthews, William, date.
  Time & money : new poems / William Matthews.
    p.   cm.
  ISBN 0-395-71134-7
  I. Title.
  PS3563.A855T56   1995
  811'.54 — dc20   95-9784   CIP

Printed in the United States of America

QUM 10 9 8 7 6 5 4 3 2

Book design by Melodie Wertelet

Some of these poems first appeared, sometimes in a different form and/or under a different title, in the following magazines. Thanks to them all.

The American Voice: "House Sitting," "A Night at the Opera," "Tomorrow," "Wasps"; *Antaeus*: "Cancer Talk," "Cellini's Chicken," "Mingus in Diaspora"; *The Atlantic Monthly*: "The Bear at the Dump," "Cheap Seats, the Cincinnati Gardens, Professional Basketball, 1959"; *Columbia*: "Babe Ruth at the End"; *crazyhorse*: "Self Help"; *Denver Quarterly*: "Social Notes from All Over: Mt. Olympus"; *Gettysburg*: "My Father's Body," "The Wolf of Gubbio"; *New England Review*: "Note Left for Gerald Stern in an Office I Borrowed, and He Would Next, at a Summer Writers' Conference"; *The New Yorker*: "Grief," "Landscape with Onlooker," "*Va, Pensiero*"; *The Ohio Review*: "Men at My Father's Funeral," "The Rented House in Maine," "A Tour of the Gardens," "Well, You Needn't"; *Passages North*: "It," "Money," "Negligence"; *Pivot*: "Pavarotti in Transport, 1990"; *Ploughshares*: "Bob Marley's Hair," "New Folsom Prison," "Old Folsom Prison," "President Reagan's Visit to New York, October 1984"; *Poetry*: "The Hour," "Last Words," "Mingus at The Showplace," "Time"; *Poetry Miscellany*: "Home Away from Home"; *Shenandoah*: "The Generations," "The Rookery at Hawthornden"; *Tar River Poetry*: "Mingus at The Half Note"

"My Father's Body" reappeared in *The Pushcart Prize: The Best of the Small Presses, 1992–1993* (Wainscott, N.Y.: Pushcart Press, 1993).

"Note Left for Gerald Stern in an Office I Borrowed, and He Would Next, at a Summer Writers' Conference" reappeared in *The Pushcart Prize: The Best of the Small Presses 1993–1994* (Wainscott, N.Y.: Pushcart Press, 1994).

Thanks for a PSC-CUNY summer grant (1990) that helped fuel my work on these poems.

FOR PAT

Brava!

The civil fiction, the calico idea,
The Johnsonian composition, abstract man,
All are evasions like a repeated phrase,
Which, by its repetition, comes to bear
A meaning without a meaning.

WALLACE STEVENS

One never knows, do one?

FATS WALLER

Contents

III

I

Mingus at The Showplace

I was miserable, of course, for I was seventeen,
and so I swung into action and wrote a poem,

and it was miserable, for that was how I thought
poetry worked: you digested experience and shat

literature. It was 1960 at The Showplace, long since
defunct, on West 4th St., and I sat at the bar,

casting beer money from a thin reel of ones,
the kid in the city, big ears like a puppy.

And I knew Mingus was a genius. I knew two
other things, but as it happened they were wrong.

So I made him look at the poem.
"There's a lot of that going around," he said,

and Sweet Baby Jesus he was right. He glowered
at me but he didn't look as if he thought

bad poems were dangerous, the way some poets do.
If they were baseball executives they'd plot

to destroy sandlots everywhere so that the game
could be saved from children. Of course later

that night he fired his pianist in mid-number
and flurried him from the stand.

"We've suffered a diminuendo in personnel,"
he explained, and the band played on.

One night shy of full, fat as a beach ball, the moon
looks not lonesome shining through the trees, but replete

with the thoughtless sensuality of well-being.
A chill in the air? No, under the air, like water

under a swimmer. The unsteadfast leaves grow crisp
and brittle, the better to fall away. Some nights

fear, like rising water in a well, fills these hours —
the dead of night, as the phrase goes, when you quicken

and the dank metallic sweat beads like a vile dew.
But tonight you stand at your window, framed and calm,

and the air's as sweet as a freshly peeled orange.
There's a moon on the lake, and another in the sky.

The Bear at the Dump

Amidst the too much that we buy and throw
away and the far too much we wrap it in,
the bear found a few items of special
interest — a honeydew rind, a used tampon,
the bone from a leg of lamb. He'd rock back
lightly onto his rear paws and slash
open a plastic bag, and then his nose —
jammed almost with a surfeit of rank
and likely information, for he would pause —
and then his whole dowsing snout would
insinuate itself a little way
inside. By now he'd have hunched his weight
forward slightly, and then he'd snatch it back,
trailed by some tidbit in his teeth. He'd look
around. What a good boy am he.
The guardian of the dump was used
to this and not amused. "He'll drag that shit
every which damn way," he grumbled
who'd dozed and scraped a pit to keep that shit
where the town paid to contain it.
The others of us looked and looked. "City
folks like you don't get to see this often,"
one year-round resident accused me.
Some winter I'll bring him down to learn
to love a rat working a length of subway
track. "Nope," I replied. Just then the bear
decamped for the woods with a marl of grease
and slather in his mouth and on his snout,
picking up speed, not cute (nor had he been
cute before, slavering with greed, his weight
all sunk to his seated rump and his nose stuck
up to sift the rich and fetid air, shaped
like a huge, furry pear), but richly
fed on the slow-simmering dump, and gone
into the bug-thick woods and anecdote.

First they take it away,
for now the body belongs to the state.
Then they open it
to see what may have killed it,
and the body had arteriosclerosis
in its heart, for this was an inside job.
Now someone must identify the body
so that the state may have a name
for what it will give away,
and the funeral people come in a stark car
shaped like a coffin with a hood
and take the body away,
for now it belongs to the funeral people
and the body's family buys it back,
though it lies in a box at the crematorium
while the mourners travel and convene.
Then they bring the body to the chapel, as they call it,
of the crematorium, and the body lies in its box
while the mourners enter and sit
and stare at the box, for the box
lies on a pedestal where the altar would be
if this were a chapel.
A rectangular frame with curtains at the sides
rises from the pedestal,
so that the box seems to fill a small stage,
and the stage gives off the familiar
illusion of being a box with one wall torn away
so that we may see into it,
but it's filled with a box we can't see into.
There's music on tape and a man in a robe
speaks for a while and I speak
for a while and then there's a prayer
and then we mourners can hear the whir
of a small motor and curtains slide
across the stage. At least for today,

I think, this is the stage that all the world is,
and another motor hums on
and we mourners realize that behind
the curtains the body is being lowered,
not like Don Giovanni to the flames
but without flourish or song
or the comforts of elaborate plot,
to the basement of the crematorium,
to the mercies of the gas jets
and the balm of the conveyer belt.
The ashes will be scattered,
says a hushed man in a mute suit,
in the Garden of Remembrance,
which is out back.
And what's left of a mild, democratic man
will sift in a heap with the residue of others,
for now they all belong to time.

Record Lows, Iowa

The cold makes the dog seem to bark
into a barrel. Northwest winds scour
the plains at twenty miles an hour,
not to count gusts. And next the dark

will shrink the circle of the world
all to this dot, this house. Frost scrims
the windows, through which who'd look in?
Light blooms from bulbs and heat unfurls

from baseboards. Through similar nights
our ancestors cringed in dank cubes
of root-woven sod like fox cubs
in a den, their hearts sped by fright

that grew usual the longer
frost gnawed toward them through the sod.
"A mighty fortress is our God,"
they sang, and the winds blew stronger.

Last Words

It wasn't Oscar Wilde who said, "Die, my dear
doctor, that's the last thing I shall do," but
Lord Palmerston. Wilde said, "Either this wall-

paper goes or I do." William Pitt said,
"Oh my country! How I leave my country!"
or, in an alternate version, "I think

I could eat one of Bellamy's veal pies."
Everyone dies alone, according to
the tough-guy swagger, though none who made it

into *Bartlett's* did. Gather witnesses.
Some may serve as straight men. "May God forgive
you," a French priest intoned, but the urbane

corpse-to-be waved him off. "Of course He will;
it's His *métier*." And there's someone whose
job it proved to remember those last words.

Someone else lit a candle by Voltaire's
bed and he raised an eyelid: "Flames, already?"
Memorability comes by practice,

but you can be too ready, as Henry
James was. "Here it is," he said, "at last,
the distinguished thing," and then lived long

to think what a shapely phrase he'd spilled.
Study the masters is, as usual, the best
advice. Or you could try the worn nostrum

laconic nineteenth-century mothers
gave their daughters for wedding nights. "Relax.
You'll think of something. Let nature take its course."

Time

I did but taste a little honey
with the end of the rod that was
in mine hand, and, lo, I must die.
                    1 Samuel 14:43

Not *sated* first, then *sad* (the two words branch,
not far apart, from the same Indo-
European root), but kindled by longing,
you amble to the window and look out.
You feel like fire's held breath just before
fire flares out from matter, but no flare comes.
And look, a blurred oval, a ghostly kiss
has formed on the window from the breath you
didn't hold. You've got time on your hands; you've
been caught red-handed with the blues and by

the worst detective in the world, yourself.
"It was blind luck, really. I knew his next
failure to move, each mope, each sullen shrug.
I knew his thoughts as if they were my own."
Cameras flash; shutters fall like tiny
guillotines. "I don't know how. Goethe said,
If I knew myself, I'd run." Of course I
didn't, and that's what broke the case open.
Only one paper used the Goethe quote:
MYSTERY WOMAN HAUNTS SELF-KNOWLEDGE CASE,

the headline blared. The article gave her
name as Gerta. "About this Swiss beauty,
nothing else is known." The time had come
(but from where? hadn't it been here always?)
for me to forgo my lush indolence.

There are places things go to be forgot:
the tip of the tongue, the back of the mind,
retirement colonies like the Linger
Longer Mobile Home Park, and memory.
Perhaps I should plan how to spend my

time, but wouldn't that, like a home movie,
prove but a way to waste the same time twice?
Maybe time's just one more inexact way
to gauge loss? But we keep more than we think.
Suppose a TV signal adventures
for years in space, then hits something solid
and adventures back. You've dozed off in front
of your TV — you've been wasting some time —
and see on the screen not flickering blue
snow but the test pattern of an El

Paso station twenty-nine years defunct,
stark as a childhood taunt or remembered
genitals. What steady company you have:
you got losses like these, you'll need two trucks
next time you move. You couldn't bear to throw
them out, you said (remember?). And now what have
you got? A gorged attic like a head cold,
a basement clogged by waste. You can't "save time"
this way or any. Nor, since it can't be
owned, can it be stolen, though afternoon

adulterers add to the tryst's fevers —
the codes and lies, the sunlight sieved by blinds,
the blank sheets and the ink at brim — the pleased
guilt of having stolen time. What might they
do for time, those from whom it got stolen?

They bowl, they shop, they masturbate before
a nap (a spot of body work at O'
Nan's Auto Service), they finish their day's
work. To begin thinking about time, we might
take all the verbs we like to think we do

to time, and turn those verbs on us, and say
that time wastes us, and time saves and buys us,
that time spends us, and time marks and kills us.
We live as the direct object of verbs
we hoped we could command. Grammar school, they called
it, and we couldn't wait to graduate.
We puffed ourselves up like a cat striving
sideways to look vast, or people who like
to be right (may God thicken their tongues, or if
they write, explode their pens). Now critics write

of my "mature work" (When, the petulant boy
in me wants to know, will they publish theirs?),
and my male friends my age and I
scan the obits every day. The word
"time" now seems, often enough, the nickname
for the phrase "time left." Suppose I didn't
go from the paper to my desk. Instead
I chaperoned my tumor every
day to radiology by subway
and rancored home with it by bus. Suppose

my job was to be nauseated and bald
from chemotherapy and still to make
the plucky joke when Procter & Gamble
sent me, "Resident," a beauty about whom
nothing else was known, hair-care products.

"Luster," the prose whispered, and "sheen." My head
looked like an egg and the prose said "coupon."
I'd have ceased calling my anxious frets about
the future "thought." On Tuesday I'd wake up
and I'd say "Tuesday," my whole essay on time.

I think that's what I'd do. I'd soldier through
the fear and fell depressions. I'd call on
what those critics like nicely to call "wit,"
i.e., the whole compressed force of my rage
and love. I'd invent whatever it took
to get me through or dead, whichever came
first. And yet we must remember this:
dire time hectors us along with it, and so
we might consider thanks. Wednesday. Thursday.
Thus water licks its steady way through stone.

Wasps

First he yelped, and then my father sprinted
the length of the tenth hole at Southern Pines
backwards, green to tee, trailing a loud plume
of wasps, slapping himself, jockey and horse.
It took more than four hundred yards before
the last vendetta wasp that had not stung

him veered off and flew back to base. We trudged
warily back to the tenth green, of course,
and putted out, then finished the back nine
while surly welts bloomed on his neck and arms.
"They're not individuals," he complained.
What was I to golf, or golf to me?

I played to keep my father's company.
"They're cells. The nest is the real animal."
I pictured their papery cone and tried
to think what the dark surge wasps passed from each
to each inside might be except the fierce
electricity of state, or family.

President Reagan's Visit to New York, October 1984

Pomp churned through midtown like a combine,
razing a path to the Waldorf-Astoria.
At 34th and 10th a black man

drizzled a wan froth of soap and dirt
on my windshield and paused for me to pay
to get it squeegeed off. He just wanted,

he said, to make an honest living.
I gave a dollar and he gave thanks; we
knew the going rate, and so we went,

but only a few feet. The light shone red.
The Waldorf bellboys (ages 23–
59) waited, too, and men in shades

and shiny suits with walkie-talkies
along the route the limousine would take.
Our creamiest streets were cordoned off so

Pomp could clot them, and the walkie-talkies
sputtered each to each. What had the black man
or I to do with this peacockery?

The light turned green. Under a soot-slurred sky
we gave each other a parting glance.
What nation you can build on that, was ours.

Two dozen bars or so into "Better Get It
in Your Soul," the band mossy with sweat,
May 1960 at The Half Note, the rain
on the black streets outside
dusted here and there by the pale pollen
of the streetlights. Blue wreaths
of smoke, the excited calm
of the hip in congregation, the long
night before us like a view and Danny
Richmond so strung out the drums
fizz and seethe. "Ho, hole, hode it,"
Mingus shouts, and the band clatters
to fraught silence. There's a twinge
in the pianist's shoulder, but this time
Mingus focuses like a nozzle
his surge of imprecations on a sleek
black man bent chattering across
a table to his lavish date:
"This is your heritage and if you
don' wanna listen, then you got
someplace else you'd better be."
The poor jerk takes a few beats
to realize he'll have to leave
while we all watch before another
note gets played. He glowers dimly
at Mingus, like throwing a rock
at a cliff, then offers his date
a disdained arm, and they leave in single
file (she's first) and don't
look back, nor at each other.
"Don' let me constrain you revellers,"
Mingus says, and then, tamed by his own rage
for now, he kick-starts the band:
"One, two, one two three four."

Few gods had jobs. They inherited not money
but all the time in the world.
Yet the cripple, Hephaestus, armorer
to the gods, set up red shop every day

on a volcano floor. He seared and clanged,
he thrust a rose sword hilt-deep into hissing
water, and billowed steam fumed back at him:
matter and energy had made an exchange.

Gods who were out of work cross-dressed as mortals
and ran each other through at leisure
and no black mist swirled up to fell them like a seizure.
They stood their airy ground and chortled,

then sprawled like fallen olivewood
and drank nectar. This is the life, they thought,
although of course it wasn't. For soot,
they had but air; for soil, the curdled clouds;

for company, each other. These bare raptures
they passed back and forth like scrip while blood choked
Troy, and Hephaestus limped and swore and stoked
his fires, ever busy filling orders.

Pavarotti in Transport, 1990

(Un Ballo in Maschera)

The knee had got so bad that when he fell,
stabbed by his best friend, in the third act,
it took four burly pages to wrest him

to the throne where he'd pardon his friend
(*No, no, lasciatelo! lasciatelo!*),
then die and loose grief like a frenzy

in the ballroom. They'd hoisted him like a big
table, one to a corner, great Riccardo.
The stem of breath climbed surely in his throat

and practice bloomed. (This is the way
we'd die, if we could choose, not sawing back
and forth on the knot with a dulling rasp

of last breath, but giving the spent soul up
like a ball held aloft by a fountain.
Surrounded by friends, shrouded by applause.)

Then the king died. *Notte, notte d'orror*,
the chorus keened, and then the curtain fell,
and the shouts and yelps and bravos rose.

Righted, he gimped out for curtain calls,
his papal stage-smile seemingly unstrained.
Backstage an hour later I watched four

stagehands, one at each corner, heft him
down the hall, his face taut with pain,
and dock him in the rear of a limousine.

Men at My Father's Funeral

The ones his age who shook my hand
on their way out sent fear along
my arm like heroin. These weren't
men mute about their feelings,
or what's a body language for?

And I, the glib one, who'd stood
with my back to my father's body
and praised the heart that attacked him?
I'd made my stab at elegy,
the flesh made word: the very spit

in my mouth was sour with ruth
and eloquence. What could be worse?
Silence, the anthem of my father's
new country. And thus this babble,
like a dial tone, from our bodies.

Old Folsom Prison

This could be Scotland: a crag and far below
the froth-marled river. Where is the stag,
the laird, where are the baying hounds?

Welcome instead to Hotel California.
Johnny Cash sang right there, in Graystone
Chapel, and from the blue, disconsolate

congregation he drew, like blood, whoops
and yelps enough to flood the place.
Rapists rose; and arsonists; and the man

who drew five life sentences, without
parole, for vehicular homicide
(a mother and four kids), to be served

consecutively, rose also; as did
murderers enough to still all breath
in a small town; and armed robbers; and

sellers of dope to your children and mine,
and earlier, perhaps, to you and me.
And when Cash sang that he'd stabbed

a man just to watch him die, their shout
rose like so many crows you'd wonder where
there was room for air, if you were there.

New Folsom Prison

Heat sensors, cameras on automatic
pan, vast slabs of prefabricated wall
trucked in and joined on site like grandiose

dominos . . . It took the state eight years
to plan to keep those men apart from you
and me and only sometimes from each other,

for even gang-rapists and murderers
are social animals. One told me, "I belong."
He'd checked his math twelve years of nights

and he belonged. "They tell you how and where
this place was built?" he asked. They couldn't stop;
they told me six times. He knew that I knew,

but neither of us let on, for we had,
the ironist and the killer, begun
to talk, for neither of us was *they*.

"No," I said. "Think," he said. "They'd need," I tried,
"cheap labor." He smiled. "Where would they get it?"
Our catechism led us straight to what

we knew. "Eureka, motherfuck," we didn't shout,
but told each other how inmates elsewhere
in the California prison system

built New Folsom part by part, day by day,
and then lay down at night in their slim bunks
to dream of violence and manufacture.

II

Along this path Ben Jonson rode to visit
William Drummond. What fun those two dour
poets must have made for one another.
Under a sycamore Drummond waited.
"Welcome, royal Ben."
                              "Greetings, Hawthornden."
The good fellowship of poets always
has, like death jokes on the eve of battle,
gravel in its craw.
                              Back from Bonnyrigg
I've come with a liter of the Famous
Grouse for my room. The six weeks I have here
to read, to write, to amble and to fester
with solitude, a slut for company
and bearing like a saucer of water
my intimates, my bawds, my pretty ones,
the words I wrote that didn't mutiny —
six such weeks are hard to find, and hard
to fill. Who scrawled between pastoral poems
a few rude lines to warn us? The blotched, mottled
sky above the glen, the rain, the rusty fox,
the melodious gargle of Scots talk,
the pale scumbled blue forget-me-nots —
all these can be but a reminder that
the world's a poem we'll not learn how to write.
Not portly Horace on his Sabine Farm,
that Yaddo-for-one, nor all the English
poets who admired but never sheared a sheep
nor steered a plow through soil's dun bilge and shoals
of stone.
                              Yet from the rookery the shrill
inventions rise. From the entire black bell

of each bird the rasped song clappers forth.
Verse is easy and poetry is hard.
The brash choir, like a polyphonic heart,
beats loudly in the trees and does not ask
what poetry can do, infamous for making
nothing happen. The rooks and I rejoice
not to be mute. The day burgeons with raucous
song about the joy of a song-stuffed throat.

Note Left for Gerald Stern in an Office I Borrowed, and He Would Next, at a Summer Writers' Conference

Welcome, good heart. I hope you like — I did —
the bust of Schiller, the reproduction
of Caspar David Friedrich's painting
of Coleridge, with his walking stick, gazing
over the peaks of German thought (the Grand
Teutons?), and the many Goethe pinups.
The life of the mind is celebrated here,

so why's the place so sad? I hate the way
academic life can function as a sort
of methadone program for the depressed,
keeping the inmates steadily fatigued
and just morose enough that a day's full
measure of glum work gets done. Cowbirds
like us will have to put in our two weeks' worth

before the studied gloom begins to leak
forth from the files, the books, the post cards sent
back by colleagues from their Fulbright venues,
Tübingen, Dubrovnik, Rome, and Oslo.
Of course our own offices wait for us
and fall is coming on. To teach, Freud warned,
is one of three impossible jobs

(the others are to govern and to cure).
To teach what you know — laughter, ignorance,
curiosity, and the erotic thrall
of work as a restraint against despair —
comes as close to freedom as anyone pays
wages for. Outside the classroom such brave words
ring dully, for failures of tolerance

coat the halls as plaque clogs an artery.
Cruelty doesn't surprise a human
much, but the drenched-in-sanctimony prose

by which the cruel christen cruelty
with a better name should rot in the mouths
of the literate. The louder they quote
Dr. Johnson, the faster I count the spoons.

Well, the grunts always kvetch about the food
and the rank morals of their officers.
Who'd want to skip that part? In the office,
though, alone with the books, post cards, busts,
and sentimental clutter, we feel rage
subside and joy recede. These dusty keepsakes
block from view the very love they're meant to be

an emblem of, the love whose name is books.
Suppose we'd been kidnapped by the space
people and whisked around the galaxies,
whirred past wonders that would render Shakespeare
mute and make poor stolid Goethe whimper
like a beagle. The stellar dust, debris
agleam in the black light, the fell silence,

the arrogantly vast scale of the creation,
the speed of attack and decay each blurred,
incised impression made, the sure greed
we'd feel to describe our tour, and how we'd fail
that greed . . . And then we're back, alone
not with the past but with how fast the past
eludes us, though surely, friend, we were there.

Self Help

It would be good to feel good about yourself for good.
The air is slurred, the seas are fouled, and the body
and soul wrangle constantly, like Freud and Jung

in their endless duet from *Il Cuore in Maschera*.
Can it be that fully and accurately to throb, woofer
and tweeter pulsating as one, with your own emotions

is the fullest expression of the life force,
or whichever whispers over the dark waters set all
this lavish and heartbreaking fuss in motion? There must be

some higher purpose to whose faint signal you could,
so to speak, tune yourself in. You'd need ears like a pair
of vacuum cleaners. Maybe the static and dry-icy gossip

of space would come to seem comforting, and the anomalous
noises, such as the one that sounded like the thinnest film
of foil, as long as a galaxy perhaps, being unwrinkled

for recycling, would also seem comforting, like a dial
tone: the line's open, though the higher purposes are away
from their desks. Despite the expense and crimped ear,

you would stay on the line, steadfast and unnumbable,
alert for the faintest bruit; might not the most minuscule
dapples of sound turn out to be duff-begrimed specklets

of instruction? You want to be one on whom nothing
was lost, but space never sleeps and you do, adrift,
with a dark and a lit side, and a noiseless momentum.

But wait. At last there's a message, faint as the rasp
of a match being struck on the bottom of a well, and it's
for you. Eat less flesh. Compare yourself carefully

to your neighbor. Don't tread on me. Let there be ego
where once there was id. Know what free advice is worth.
God weeps for the helpless, and without a sound.

Babe Ruth at the End

The press loved him, of course.
After one game somebody wrote,
"Babe Ruth was not able
to make any home runs."
How about Ruth's roommate?
Wouldn't that make a story?
So they asked Ping Brodie
and he said, "I don't room with him.
I room with his suitcase."
He was out eating ribs

or some bimbo. Earlier
he'd stood in front of the hotel,
the winecask of his upper
body furred by camel's hair,
a camel's hair cap aslant
on his head, and his deft nose
sifted the night air for lures.
On those spindle legs he stole
in his first four Yankee seasons
fifty bases. This genial slob

and imperious infant had
a disguise for his stealth,
and, like yours or mine,
it was his personality.
No matter that he barely hid
his life: cancer, that savage
biographer, riddled the Babe's
ample, only, and supple body,
and at last he lay like a balloon
leaking air on his hospital bed,

and Connie Mack, baseball's
Calvin Coolidge, last man
to manage in a suit, came to see
the Babe, baseball's Teddy Roosevelt,
on his deathbed. "Hello, Mr. Mack.
The termites have got me." History
has held Mack's tongue as easily
as it loosed Ruth's. What would you
have said, if you were Mack, or Ruth?
Something you already knew?

Cheap Seats, the Cincinnati Gardens,
Professional Basketball, 1959

The less we paid, the more we climbed. Tendrils
of smoke lazed just as high and hung there, blue,
particulate, the opposite of dew.
We saw the whole court from up there. Few girls
had come, few wives, numerous boys in molt
like me. Our heroes leapt and surged and looped
and two nights out of three, like us, they'd lose.
But "like us" is wrong: we had no result
three nights out of three: so we had heroes.
And "we" is wrong, for I knew none by name
among that hazy company unless
I brought her with me. This was loneliness
with noise, unlike the kind I had at home
with no clock running down, and mirrors.

Rather than hold his hands properly
arched off the keys, like cats
with their backs up,
Monk, playing block chords,
hit the keys with his fingertips well
above his wrists,

shoulders up, wrists down, scarce
room for the pencil, ground
freshly to a point,
piano teachers love to poke
into the palms of junior
pianists with lazy hands.

What easy villains these robotic
dullards are in their floral-
print teaching dresses
(can those mauve blurs be
peonies?). The teachers' plucky,
make-do wardrobes suggest, like the wan

bloom of dust the couch exhaled
when I scrunched down to wait
for Mrs. Oxley, just how we value
them. She'd launch my predecessor
home and drink some lemonade,
then free me from the couch.

The wisdom in Rocky Mount,
North Carolina, where Monk grew up,
is that those names, Thelonious
Sphere, came later, but nobody's
sure: he made his escape
by turning himself into a genius

in broad daylight while nobody
watched. Just a weird little black
kid one day and next thing anybody
knew he was inexplicable
and gone. We don't give lessons
in that. In fact it's to stave off

such desertions that we pay
for lessons. It works for a while.
Think of all the time we spend
thinking about our kids.
It's Mrs. Oxley, the frump
with a metronome, and Mr. Mote,

the bad teacher and secret weeper,
we might think on, and everyone
we pay to tend our young, opaque
and truculent and terrified,
not yet ready to replace us,
or escape us, if that be the work.

It

What was it? Whatever it was, it stood
for itself: it wasn't a pronoun. It
held — no, it was — the center of the room
in which we sat to talk about it

in a circle. "What is it like?" someone
asked. And someone said, "It's ineffable";
and someone asked, "What's ineffable mean?"
"It means you can't eff it," said someone else.

"And you can't see it," another said, "and you
can't be it." That was talk. Then: silence — drear,
mineral, and like a dusk made not from
dark and light but from will and sleep — had run
through us its alternating current, fear
and hope. We sat. What else was there to do?

In the Boathouse

Reflected light — it had leaked in between
the planks — freckled the walls. "Kiss me," she'd say.
The boat swayed under us. Raptly we grazed
on one another's mouths, as if to eat

hunger and be filled. And then she'd take my
livid cock in her deft fist and slowly coax
me to erupt. Next she'd delve in her purse
for an embroidered handkerchief and wipe

me dry. She wore no underpants and brought
her purse with a fresh linen handkerchief
each afternoon. She had such frank mischief
in her eyes, she lowered them to say, "Now,

kiss me somewhere else." A stern friend accused
me: "It's only physical, right?" Well, yes,
like a cloud or marmot, like the nervous
system, like the world whose famous beauty

is but skin-deep. And from the lush blossom
of her brain to the heart's southernmost tip,
Cape Clitoris, and to her toes, the spirit
lolled in its sticky flesh, its kingdom come.

III

Negligence

A woman opens a parcel with no
return address. Last month her only son
drove himself full tilt into a maple
and each day brings new drudgery from grief.
What's this? A vase, an urn? Off with its lid.
And so she's up to her wrists in her son's
ashes — not, by the way, like silt or dust,
but nubble and grit, boneshards and half-burnt
burls of cartilage, cinders and nuggets.
I ask you, ladies and gentlemen
of the jury, to glove her hands with yours
and sieve the rubble of your beloved
only son, and also I ask you this:
what simple task could the funeral home
perform to run this cruel film backwards,
to lift this woman's hands from the cinders
of her son and wind them back to her slack
lap, and why did these merchants of balm
fail to perform it? I believe you know
as well as I that it takes but paltry
seconds more to write a return address
than to endorse a check. It's easy to say
what they ought to have done, and did not do.
What's hard to know is how to value grief.
It's very hard — but it's the very job
you're here to do. You have to ask and ask,
Could this grief have been prevented? until you
answer. Money may seem a crude measure
in philosophy, though it seems exact
enough for the grocer's and mortician's
bills.
        I beg your pardon, Your Honor.
I meant but to say that a jury's duty

is to blame or not to blame,
                              and if there's
fault there's got to be a reason for it,
and so a price for reason. What's honor
worth that's ladled like soup onto plates, all
the slosh that fits and then no more? Suppose
you pulled into a gas station and asked
for a full tank. "How far you gonna go?"
"Twelve miles east of Bozeman." "Then half a tank
will do." A freak mishap (golf course, four iron,
lightning) is one thing, and preventable
heartbreak another. This woman's bruised heart
is evidence, ladies and gentlemen
of the jury, and this plain brown paper
with no return address. If there's excuse
for every harm, what use then is law?
Ladies and gentlemen of the jury, I ask
you to vote against random pain, to vote
that suffering has cause and thus has blame,
to vote that our lives can be explained, and
to vote compensation for my client.

The Rented House in Maine

At dawn, the liquid clatter of rain
pocks the bay and stutters on the roof.
Even when it's this gray, the first slant light
predicts across the rug gaunt shadows
of the generic paper birds
my landlord's pasted to the eastern wall,

all glass, to fend specific birds
from bonking themselves dull or worse
against the bright blare of false sky.
From the bay the house must look
like a grade-school homeroom gussied up
for parents' night. I like to build

a small fire first thing in the morning,
drink some coffee, drive to town,
buy the *Times*, drive back to embers
the color of canned tomato soup
(made not with water but with milk).
In this house I fell — no, hurled myself —

in love, and elsewhere, day by day,
it didn't last. Tethered to lobster traps,
buoys wobble on the bay. On the slithering
surface of the water, the rain seems
to explode — chill shrapnel, and I look
away. Embers and cool coffee. Matter,

energy, the speed of light: the universe
can be explained by an equation. Everything
that goes from one side of the equal sign
is exactly replaced from the other; i.e.,
nothing much happens at a speed so fast
we scarcely notice it, but so steadily

the math always checks out. This is thought
as I know and love it. Why did that marriage
fail? I know the reasons and count the ways.
The clouds with squalls in their cheeks,
like chaws or tongues, have broken up.
The fire is down, the coffee cold, the sun is up.

Mingus in Diaspora

You could say, I suppose, that he ate his way out,
like the prisoner who starts a tunnel with a spoon,
or you could say he was one in whom nothing was lost,
who took it all in, or that he was big as a bus.

He would say, and he did, in one of those blurred
melismatic slaloms his sentences ran — for all
the music was in his speech: swift switches of tempo,
stop-time, double time (he could *talk* in 6/8),

"I just ruined my body." And there, Exhibit A,
it stood, that Parthenon of fat, the tenant voice
lifted, as we say, since words are a weight, and music.
Silence is lighter than air, for the air we know

rises but to the edge of the atmosphere.
You have to pick up The Bass, as Mingus called
his, with audible capitals, and think of the slow years
the wood spent as a tree, which might well have been

enough for wood, and think of the skill the bassmaker
carried without great thought of it from home
to the shop and back for decades, and know
what bassists before you have played, and know

how much of this is stored in The Bass like energy
in a spring and know how much you must coax out.
How easy it would be, instead, to pull a sword
from a stone. But what's inside the bass wants out,

the way one day you will. Religious stories are rich
in symmetry. You must release as much of this hoard
as you can, little by little, in perfect time,
as the work of the body becomes a body of work.

A Tour of the Gardens

The villa itself is private, the guidebook
says, but the substantial gardens (one star)
may be viewed 11–13, closed
Mondays and August. What the book won't say
is that the Count now and then entertains
himself by meeting tourists at the gate
and taking them around the topiary,
down the avenue of umbrella pines
to the geometrical explosion
of bloom at the garden's bottom,
to stare out over the ancestral plantings
of vines and olives and fruit and nut trees.
Here everyone is silent. We slowly
turn away and start the muffled trudge
back to the gate. A woman in pale lime-
colored slacks mutters, not softly,
the word "breeding," and the affable Count,
walking backwards, addressing us all, says,
"The mystique of breeding is crucial
to us aristocrats, for if good manners
and a seemly restraint of insolence
can be learned diligently in one
generation, then our women need not be
covered like brood mares, and our bloodlines
are merely family history, the dullest
form of gossip." And now we're at the gate.
"Without the mystique of breeding," he says,
closing the gate, "I'd need another job,
and you'd need to decide if wealth itself
were not the node, the very heart, of what
you've come so far, and paid so much, to see."

The Hour

A cat came round the shed
with tail erect, but no one else was there.
Blue rivulets of shadow — these from some
tatty mullein stems — trickled steadily

across the snowcrust. I'd come to spend
an hour with the hour
I'd denied, and to see what my lie bought.
We left the door ajar to fold your blue

dress over, and you crossed your spindly arms
and grasped it by the hem and pulled it,
rather slowly I thought,
over your taunting face, then stalled a beat

or two like that. I was happy beyond
explanation with our drama, so that
while you paused in a silk caesura
I insinuated,

and for this I had knelt,
my nubbled tongue into your soapy navel,
for you were fresh from the shower, and then
we were all over one another. There

would be hell to pay and hell would take a check,
but that's another story.
A lie's like having a lock on the door,
I thought the first time I told it, and soon

enough we were locked in, the lie and I.
Why would I go back to the shed? I needed
to get out: the lie and I raked at each
other's nerves. But out

is anywhere and I went to the shed
and scuffed my feet like a schoolboy and threw
a small stone at a crow and stroked the cat
and then my time was up.

Home Away from Home

Sparse mail came, no phone rang, much work got done.
A scrim of haze hung over Umbria;
a scrim of ignorance hung over me:

what paltry Italian I could speak
came from menus, wine lists, and libretti.
I knew a few imprecations. I could

fend the neighbor's gaunt cat from the doorway
because it sprayed the bedspread the one time
it slipped in, and fend it in the mother

tongue: *Basta, va, gattino perfido.*
Well then, I could harangue small animals
in a new language. I sat in the sun-

stained piazza at noon and dandled my
second cappuccino, a happy man.
Crisi nel Gulfo, brayed the papers. Stern men

lofted planes and scowled at maps. This brandish
will be war before it's over, I said
to myself in the same sage tone of voice

I hated as a boy — men over drinks
or in barbershops talked like that, who knew
how the world works, they'd have you know. And now

I'm fluent in their dialect, and I'm
right about the war, as they were always right,
and I'm as smug and helpless as they were.

When the tubes in the radio had refurled
for the night their flickering orange
filamental tongues; and when the fountain
of bedtalk he could hear through the wall
to his parents' room stopped gurgling,

so that he heard the wind, like a comb
with a few teeth broken, rake the papery corn-
stubble before it rose to roll a tattoo
against the skin of his window; then the boy
knew he was on his own, except for his

dopey kitten, Asterisk, and he grew
sore afraid. While the kitten teetered across
the headboard of his bed like a high-wire
walker, placing each paw where it had fit
easily when she'd been smaller, holding

her breath (Tuna Dinner), scrabbling across
with two near-falls, he lay face down, fingers
knit across the back of his head against
her flailing claws if she should topple, but
she had not. She sat in her Egyptian

doorstop pose at the end of the headboard.
And that meant he could see her, dimly, but
he could. The dark that had gathered itself
so casually — a swatch from under
the eaves, a tatter from the dry creekbed,

a burgeoning stain in the east near dusk
like a gaggle of gossips — suddenly
was black dye, and all the world a smother
of settling cloth from which a kitten
wriggled free, and thus a sleepless boy.

Money

"Honey, I don't want to shock you,
but white people aren't white,
they're pink," a rich man's cook
told me when I was six. She was beating
egg whites for lemon meringue pie,
which the boss loved. Well then,
I thought, I'll sing for my supper,
and it worked then, though later
I got Jell-O often, and for so
little grew rancid with charm.

I rode the bike and flung the daily
paper from it. I got the grades
and brought them home. I caught
the ball and threw it back and fed
the dog while the ball was in flight,
and didn't ask, "Have I got this right?"
There were those who were good
for nothing and I set myself apart
from them. I'd make myself at home
here, like a weevil in the flour,

or like the mouse behind the stove.
The cat that killed that mouse was so
lazy and fat that it lay before
its bowl to eat and lived to be sixteen.

I remember my first raise. I smoldered
with a stupid, durable pleasure for weeks:
this stuff is powerful, like alcohol,
I thought, but it wasn't stuff, it was numbers,
nothing more than squiggles of dried ink,
though they were like new muscles

(from the Latin *musculus*, "little
mouse," for the ripple under the skin).
There were people said to be smart about
money because they had a good supply,
like those who were known to have good taste
since they shared the taste of those who said so.
I didn't want smart, though knowledge sticks
to me like dust to a dog — I'm a kind
of intellectual Velcro. Still, I do
sniff around, because that's what I wanted,

my snout to the confounded, uric ground.
"Led by the nose," even your friends will say
if you can't, or won't, describe what you want.
Or "driven," it doesn't seem to matter
which, so long as the engine isn't you.
"A simple farmboy with a smattering
of Latin, my ass," Friend B tells Friend A.
"Did you notice the shoes on that peacock?"
Friendship, too, is a species of money.
You get what you need by never knowing

what you want; you ramble like a sentence
growing ever longer and carefully
avoiding verbs, so if you imagine
the exact verb you've got a space for it,
and the fit's so tight you'd not know

there'd ever been a gap but for the ache,
which is yours always, like a phantom limb.
If you're rich enough you can be haunted
by all the dross you ever wanted,
and if you're poor enough you itch

for money all the time and scratch yourself
with anger, or, worse, hope. These thoughts
aren't dark; they're garishly well lit. Let's see
what's on TV. The news — murder and floods
and something heartwarming about a dog —
and then a commercial, but for what?
A woman in a blue silk dress eases
into a gray sedan and swirls it through turn
after turn alongside the Pacific.
She drives it right onto the beach

while the sun subsides and the ocean laces
and unlaces at her feet. She walks and pouts,
hooking her slate-colored pumps on her
left index finger. She'll ruin her new
hose and doesn't care. She purses her bruised-fruit
lips, and the sea, like a dull dog,
brings back what we throw out. What do
we want, and how much will we pay
to find out, and how much never to know?
What's wrong with money is what's wrong with love:

it spurns those who need it most for someone
already rolling in it. But only
the idea of justice is about
being just, and it's only an idea.
Money's not an abstraction; it's math
with consequences, and if it's a kind

of poetry, it's another inexact way,
like time, to measure some sorrow we can't
name. The longer you think about
either, the stupider you get,

while dinner grows tepid and stale.
The dogs have come in like a draft
to beg for scraps and nobody's
at the table. The father works on tax forms.
The mother folds laundry and hums
something old and sweetly melancholy.
The children drift glumly towards fracas.
None of these usual doldrums will lift
for long if they sit down to dinner, but
there's hunger to mollify, and the dogs.

Private Eye

A yellow dress, a crusted spoon,
an unwatered begonia . . .
The clue's but one scrap of the world's

rich litter and you don't know which,
so you're driving west on Pico
(does Pico run west?), low on gas

and snappy patter. Who's tailing
whom, you or your venal shadow?
If you kneel to the keyhole and stare

into your own eye, you'll think, first,
"The sumbitch is kneeling, or maybe
a dwarf." And then, "So this is self-

knowledge." But it's not; it's what
you found instead. Taco-mongers
and bail-bondsmen switch off their lights.

A chartreuse Chevrolet swirls past
and from it someone yells at you:
"Go home and sleep it off, you foo . . ."

Here's the romantic loner's curse:
you can't be good until you're with
others, and then it's impossible.

Bob Marley's Hair

The dreadlocks had all fallen off
from chemotherapy. When bald
Bob Marley died in Miami
they flew the body in the hold

to Kingston, where he would lie
in state, or in the anti-state he'd
written all his hymns for, his face
ironed into repose and sweet,

or bland if sweet couldn't be done.
"Baldheads" is what Rastas call
white people. So the body needed not
just hair but the corkscrewed waterfall

in all the photographs, the coiled crown
he could fling that would spring back,
the curtain he could part or close,
his proud tatters. No wig could fake that.

In the cabin on the same flight
Marley's mother kept the dreadlocks
like a folded flag, or dog tags,
on her lap in a box.

Cellini's Chicken

"Stout as a roach," Benvenuto Cellini diagnosed
his genius proudly, and why not? It fled light
and dined on debris, and flat as a shadow it skimmed

Cellini's floors. These breadcrumbs, this chicken
breast and quarter cup of Parmesan comprise
ordinary life, as do the trucks that lug

us food and the fossil fuels that slosh and sink
in the tanks of those vast trucks — each pint
to a dinosaur as a bouillon cube is to a cow,

but smaller: think microchip. The tarry billows
above the oilfields of Kuwait are also ordinary life.
Ubi panis ibi patria: where there's bread,

there's a homeland. Can Cellini — minion, goldsmith,
and slut for commissions — really have known how
genius scuttles its way not through, but along

with, ordinary life? If a poor man eats a chicken,
the proverb goes, one of them is sick. We can throw
the bones away or, better, make stock. The pink slur

of chicken juice we forget to wipe from the cutting
board is the elixir that drives the roaches wild,
or more domestic, we're not sure which.

House Sitting

Goodbye for two weeks to the soiled, productive
city and its excellent doctors, and hello
foster cats who foam at our ankles mornings

to get fed and then like torpid clouds drift
in and out to coil and sleep and to disdain (pink
yawns, dainty shivers) how strange we smell. To lure

them in at night we bang on a catfood can
with a fork, and from memories of snakes killed
in the pachysandra and dragged like paragons

of yarn across the patio, and from
memories of shuddering under shrubs
while lightning scrawled the sky and sheared an oak

limb into the geraniums, and by
a seemly love of comfort, the cats saunter in.
The shrill, fat squirrel, sacker of birdfeeders,

snoozes high in the maple; and the strange bipeds
(one with a tumor tethered to the spine) sleep
on the second floor, cats on the first-floor couches,

and a mouse behind the stove, stowaways all.
Rain will rinse the lawn and trees, but inside
dust, the dandruff of matter, furs the house.

Dead Languages

There must be some so dead we don't

know they existed, but what we mean
by dead is: nobody speaks them anymore.

The bees that made the wax that sank
while scribes scritched late into the night,
the beekeeper, the inkmaker, whoever pared

the quilltips, and the birds who extruded
those quills and the calves who became
vellum, all these fell dead and nameless,
but the languages remain alive.

So why the name? Because what we love
in them, except for those few people who
can read Sappho or Horace well enough
to weep with pleasure, is something dead
indeed, those fossils of meaning that died

when words evolved toward something
more like what they mean today. Yes, *senile*
and *Senate* "grew" from the same "root"
(we call the dead things live, and live ones dead).
Once *disappoint* meant to turn out of office;
and *precarious* meant "depending on

prayers" (cf. *imprecate*), and still does.
And *penis* and *pencil* (women writers
won't be surprised to know) both derive
from the Indo-European *pes* ("tail"):
hence the Latin *penis* ("little tail"): hence
the drinking toast: "Here's lead in your pencil."

And *villain* once meant, simply, someone
who lived in the country, but over time
he became a rube, and then a scoundrel;
though *pentis,* a lean-to, became *penthouse.*
Live English lugs a dead language inside.

Our aspirations, fears and snobberies
got printed there sharply as trilobites.
It was first a *shoal* of fish, then "folkchanged,"
as etymologists say when they mean

we did it without thinking, to a *school.*
But we know how to choose without thinking.
We fall in love or out, we forget

to remember. We did what we did, we're
not proud nor ashamed, we led our lives

or they led us, and how would we know which?

Va, Pensiero

When Verdi lay dying, the Milanese
scattered straw for blocks around his house
to muffle the clatter of horses
so the Maestro could easily release

his breath, *piano*, no more fuss than that.
Someone reading across the room looked up:
the silence had gone slack. Soon enough,
as I thought when my father was first dead,

the consolations will begin. Time now
to spurn all balms, to hold up like a glass
of wine (*Libiamo!*) the malice
I hoarded, the blessings I held in my mouth

like spit, the spite I burnt for fuel.
Who snarls across the stage with a drawn sword;
who gives and then defiles his or her word,
unless it's me, or you? And we can't use

ever the hoard we didn't spend.
Now consolation means something.
And so three massed choirs poise to sing
Va, pensiero in February 1901.

Their visible, blobbed breath rose like a ghost
above the flower-barnacled coffin.
Fly, thought, the hymn begins, and like a falcon
thought goes, and like a falcon thought comes home.

The Generations

I've been poor, but since I'm an American
I hated it. Bills drifted through the mail
slot of the door like snow, and desperate
people who'd hired themselves out to dun
their fellow debtors phoned during dinner
to extract shame and promises from me.
"Who called, my sweet?" my wife would wanly ask.
Her hopes were dwindling for a second dress.

I'd not carried a hod, nor laid a brick,
nor tamped tar to a roof in August,
nor squeezed my body into a freshly
gouged trench in the street to thaw a city
pipe while my co-workers clomped their feet
against the cold and yelled moral support
at me. I had a typewriter and was
that dreadful thing, a serious young

literary man. The void and I stared
at each other, and I showed my throat.
In that same throat one day I'd find my voice.
I needed time, I thought, and money, too,
but I was wrong. The voice had been there all
along. I needed work that milled me
to flour and to rage. I needed to know
not only that the boss would never pay

enough, but also that if I were boss
I wouldn't pay enough unless I grew
to be a better man than I was then.
I needed not to turn my back to my
then wife and mollify, *sotto voce*
as if I were planning a tryst,
the wretch whose dire job it was to nag me.
I needed to stand short — a tiny man,

a stick figure, as my young sons, little
Shakespeares, drew me: "the poor, bare, forked
animal." Of course they draw everyone
that way, I thought, mincing garlic
one torpid afternoon, and then I saw
that they were right. Mottled by cat dander,
perfumed by peanut butter and wet sheets,
they were powerless enough to know

the radical equality of human
souls, but too coddled to know they knew it.
They could only draw it, and they blamed
their limited techniques for the great truth
that they showed, that we're made in the image
of each other and don't know it. How hard
we'll fight to keep that ignorance they had
yet to learn, and they had me as teacher.

Of course it's not on the X-rays: tumors
have no bones. But thanks to the MRI
we see its vile flag luffing from your spine.
To own a fact you buy many rumors:

is the blob benign, or metastatic
to the bone and fatal, or curable?
There will be tests. How good were you in school?
Cells are at work on your arithmetic.

You don't have to be a good soldier.
Lymphoma is exquisitely sensitive
to radiation, but it's not what you have.
How easy it once seemed to grow older.

Don't you hate the phrase "growth experience"?
Big as a grapefruit? Big as a golf ball?
You'll learn new idioms (how good in school
were you?) like "protocol" and "exit burns."

"You'll be a cure," a jaunty resident
predicts. What if you could be you, but rid
of the malignant garrison? How would
it feel to hear in your own dialect —

not Cancer Babble but clear Broken Heart?
Bald, queasy, chemotherapeutic beau-
ty, welcome home from Port-a-Cat and eu-
phemism. Let the healing candor start.

A Night at the Opera

"The tenor's too fat," the beautiful young
woman complains, "and the soprano
dowdy and old." But what if Otello's
not black, if Rigoletto's hump lists,
if airy Gilda and her entourage
of flesh outweigh the cello section?

In fairy tales, the prince has a good heart,
and so as an outward and visible
sign of an inward, invisible grace,
his face is not creased, nor are his limbs gnarled.
Our tenor holds in his liver-spotted
hands the soprano's broad, burgeoning face.

Their combined age is ninety-seven; there's
spittle in both pinches of her mouth;
a vein in his temple twitches like a worm.
Their faces are a foot apart. His eyes
widen with fear as he climbs to the high
B-flat he'll have to hit and hold for five

dire seconds. And then they'll stay in their stalled
hug for as long as we applaud. Franco
Corelli once bit Birgit Nilsson's ear
in just such a command embrace because
he felt she'd upstaged him. Their costumes weigh
fifteen pounds apiece; they're poached in sweat

and smell like fermenting pigs; their voices rise
and twine not from beauty, nor from the lack
of it, but from the hope for accuracy
and passion, both. They have to hit the note
and the emotion, both, with the one poor
arrow of the voice. Beauty's for amateurs.

"Grief": The last line of my poem translates the Dante line.

"Record Lows, Iowa": The first sentence of the poem I took from John Cheever's *Journals*.

"Bob Marley's Hair": The poem conflates details of two flights: one from Switzerland, where Marley went late in his life for alternative cancer treatment, and the flight of his body home from Miami, where he died in Cedars of Lebanon Hospital.

"*Va, Pensiero*": Verdi died on 27 January 1901, and there was a private funeral service on 30 January. The official, municipal memorial service, described in my poem, took place, after much planning, on 27 February. Eight hundred and twenty voices sang "Va, pensiero" (*Nabucco*, Act III); Maestro Toscanini conducted.